THE LAMB WILL CONQUER:
REFLECTIONS ON THE KNOCK APPARITION

Published 2017 by
Veritas Publications
7–8 Lower Abbey Street
Dublin 1
Ireland
publications@veritas.ie
www.veritas.ie

ISBN 978 1 84730 789 7

10 9 8 7 6 5 4 3 2 1

A catalogue record for this book is available from the British Library.

All scripture quotations taken from the *CTS New Catholic Bible*, Catholic
Truth Society, Publishers to the Holy See, 2007.

Designed by Padraig McCormack, Veritas Publications
Images supplied by © Knock Shrine
Printed in Ireland by KC Print, Killarney, Co. Kerry

THE LAMB WILL CONQUER

Reflections on the Knock Apparition

Nigel Woollen

VERITAS

Dedication

To all the friends of Knock Shrine,
both present and future.

Contents

Acknowledgements

With thanks to my family, to Léonie Scott-Boras for her diligent proofreading, to Anne and Paul for the use of their island retreat to write this book, and to all at Veritas for their support.

Introduction
Tear the Heavens Open!

'You're mad to go to Knock!' the kind lady said, chuckling. I was a bit taken aback. Where I come from, this means: you're crazy or stupid to go to Knock. She hastily explained that in West of Ireland parlance, it signifies: you *really want* to go to Knock – you simply can't wait to go! And indeed I couldn't. From my first visits to Ireland, this village in County Mayo has held a deep fascination for me; it's a place in which you feel at home straight away, but also sense something quite unique. There's an atmosphere of peace rarely found elsewhere, a feeling that heaven touches earth in a particular way. So, for the many of us who are 'mad to go to Knock', it's worth exploring in depth the meaning of the Knock event, to understand something of what God wanted to reveal to those witnesses of 1879, and what he wants to say to us today. 'I will hear what the Lord God has to say, a voice that speaks of peace' (Psalm 84:9).

One of the most moving prayers in the Old Testament is found near the end of the book of the prophet Isaiah: 'Oh, that you would tear the heavens open and come down – at your presence the mountains would melt – to make the nations tremble at your presence, working unexpected miracles, such as no one has ever heard of before' (Isaiah 63:29–64:3).

This prayer, expressing in the strongest terms the prophet's yearning for the Lord to reveal his presence, is radical and bold: for the people of Israel, the Lord is all-holy, utterly beyond the grasp of human beings; no one can see him and live. To ask God to reveal himself is a risk! He always answers our prayers – yet not always in the way we think: 'the heavens are as high above earth as my ways are above your ways, my thoughts above your thoughts' (Isaiah 55:9).

God will indeed reply to this ardent prayer of the prophet, in a way beyond all human logic or expectation: by the incarnation of his only Son, Jesus, born on this earth to redeem his people and to open the gates of the kingdom to the whole human race. Jesus willed to be baptised by John in the river Jordan; Mark's Gospel tells us that no sooner had Jesus come up out of the water than 'he saw the heavens torn apart and the Spirit, like a dove, descending on him. And a voice came from heaven, "You are my Son, the Beloved; my favour rests on you"' (Mark 1:10–11). God truly has torn open the heavens to send his Spirit upon his beloved Son Jesus, who will proclaim the Good News of the kingdom and perform saving works to show the Father's power. Yet his ultimate goal is to give his own life for us on the Cross; he is the sacrificial Lamb who offers his life in order to save us from sin and death, and enable us to gain access to Paradise! At the death of Jesus on the Cross, 'the veil of the Temple was torn in two from top to bottom' (Mark 15:38), a sign which seems to signify the end of Temple worship, but which also reminds us that the way has been opened to heaven: the veil of the Holy of Holies – representing the place of God's presence, that none of us can reach by our own efforts – is torn apart: we are now invited to heaven, through the sacred humanity of God's own Son. He came down to earth in order to bring us to heaven, and he himself is the Way – this is the Good News!

When we think of our poor world, in which countless innocent people suffer, and where so many of God's children do not yet know his love for them – often making destructive decisions that lead them further away from the loving Father who waits to show mercy to them – we may often be tempted to pray Isaiah's prayer once more: 'Oh, that you would tear the heavens open and come down!' Yet God continues to answer this prayer every day: whenever good people pray with faith, the heavens are opened to bring grace to our world, for 'the heartfelt prayer of a good man works very powerfully' (James 5:16). Each time a Baptism takes place, the heavens are torn open, the Spirit comes to rest on the new Christian, and the Father's voice whispers, 'You are my beloved child!' It is above all, at every Mass, that the heavens are *truly* torn open: Christ himself comes down to us. At the word of the priest, who obeys the Lord's mandate entrusted to his Church, the bread and wine are transformed into the very Body and Blood of Jesus, renewing his saving sacrifice of the Cross. He wants to give us the best food for our journey – for he is the Lamb of God who takes away our sins – by feeding us with his own self, until the day when the veil will be lifted, and we will see him as he really is, in the joy of the saints in heaven.

In the sacraments, and especially in the Eucharist, we have everything! At every Mass, we first of all express sorrow for our sins, as a community of weak, vulnerable sinners who want to grow in mercy. Then we hear the Word of God – who speaks to his children of his love – and finally receive the Word made flesh, for he doesn't merely want to speak to us but to live in us, sharing the mess of our lives in order to redeem them and turn us into something beautiful, transforming us into his very self: we are what we eat! We are then sent out to bear witness to his goodness and mercy; like the Lamb, we are blessed, broken and given, in order that the world might discover his love and turn to him in hope.

However, the Lord knows we need 'extras'. We need signs of his love that kindle in us this yearning for the kingdom, the desire that the heavens be torn open anew. Throughout Church history particular manifestations of God's presence, approved by Church authorities, have helped his pilgrim people on their journey, renewing their faith and enabling them to grow in his love. The 'unexpected miracle' (Isaiah 64:2) that took place in Knock, a small village in the west of Ireland, in 1879, when several people saw a vision – of the Lamb of God, accompanied by Our Lady, St Joseph and St John the Evangelist – on the gable wall of their parish church, is not strictly necessary for salvation; it doesn't add any new revelation to all that the Church hands down to us through Scripture and Tradition. And yet, if we believe that God always wants to speak to us, that he can tear open the heavens to shine his kindly light upon us, then we can be grateful for such an 'extra' to confirm us in our faith and help us to know something more of his wonderful love. The Knock apparition is unparalleled in Church history; although authorities have not as of yet confirmed its supernatural character, stating merely that the testimony of the fifteen witnesses was 'trustworthy and satisfactory' (in two commissions of enquiry, in 1879 and 1936) – and certainly no one is obliged to believe

THE LAMB WILL CONQUER

in any particular private revelation – however its nature is of such depth, and to this day its manifest fruits have endured so powerfully, that we cannot simply cast it aside as an irrelevance. The more we meditate on the apparition and its message, the less credible it seems that the whole scene was invented! It must be stressed that our Christian faith rests on the Word of God, not on private revelations; at the same time, authentic private revelations confirm and echo God's Word entrusted to the Church. For example, Our Blessed Mother's words to St Bernadette in Lourdes in 1858 – 'I am the Immaculate Conception' – came four years after her Immaculate Conception was dogmatically defined by Blessed Pius IX in 1854.

We can recall, too, the pilgrimage to Knock in 1979 of St John Paul II (who also meditated at length on the message of the apparition in an Angelus address during the Marian Year on 13 March 1988) which is a strong affirmation of the coherence between the silent vision a century earlier and the perennial message of the Gospel.

John the Baptist: A voice in the wilderness

A good place for visiting pilgrims to start a tour of Knock Shrine is the dedication stone of the original parish church in 1828, found on the outer wall where it now joins onto the Apparition Chapel. The then pastor, Fr P. O'Grady, chose two biblical citations for this dedication stone: 'My House shall be called the House of Prayer to all Nations' (Mark 11:17) and 'This is the gate of the Lord; the just shall enter it' (Psalm 117:20). This is prophecy in action! Surely no one could have imagined – at a time of great poverty and persecution – that pilgrims would come from all nations to this obscure village in a remote corner of Ireland, in order to pray, so that his house could truly be a house of prayer. And the 'gate' of Psalm 117 – which joyfully sings the Lord's praise as pilgrims enter solemnly into the Temple – can be understood as our 'gateway' to heaven, won for us by the Passion of Christ, who fulfils the Psalms and every part of the Old Covenant (Luke 24:44).

There's more: that same pastor, over fifty years before the apparition, was inspired to dedicate the new church to St John the Baptist! Why not, you might ask? Any saint will do … Well, think about who the Baptist is: Jesus' older cousin, who leaps for joy in his mother's womb at the coming of the Lord (Luke 1:41); he exclaims, when he sees Jesus coming towards him, 'Look, there is the Lamb of God that takes away the sin of the world!' (John 1:29) He baptises Jesus in the Jordan, when the heavens are torn open (see above); the Lord praises John saying, 'of all the children born of women, a greater than John the Baptist has never been seen' and also calls him the new Elijah (Matthew 11:11,14), the prophet who called down the fire of the Lord on the sacrifice at Mount Carmel (1 Kings 18:20–40) and who was to return, as the Jews believed, in the Messianic era. Finally, the Baptist is imprisoned and put to death by Herod for defending the sanctity of marriage (Mark 6:17–29) – he's not just any old saint!

So the saint who proclaimed the Lamb of God, who baptised our Lord – thus causing the heavens to be torn open – was chosen as patron saint of the parish church in front of which, fifty-one years later, the Lamb appeared. There's another aspect to consider: Mark in his Gospel prefaces the appearance of John the Baptist by quoting Isaiah: 'A voice cries in the wilderness: Prepare a way for the Lord, make his paths straight' (Isaiah 40:3), before announcing, 'John the Baptist appeared in the wilderness, proclaiming a Baptism of repentance for the forgiveness of sins' (Mark 1:3–4).

The wilderness, or desert, is a key place in God's revelation. The Hebrew word for wilderness is *midbar*, literally, a 'place without words', a place of silence. In the wonderful irony of salvation history, it was during the Israelites' forty years in the wilderness, the place without words, that God gave the

Decalogue, the Ten Words or Commandments to Moses (Exodus 20). Now, in the silence of the desert, the voice of the prophet resounds powerfully, calling his people to repent, to change their way of thinking, in order that their hearts be ready to welcome the one who is to come. Finally, it is to the wilderness that Jesus, the very Word of God, goes – immediately after his baptism by John – for forty days, to prepare himself for his mission, and also, surely, to show us the way to prepare for our mission of spreading the good word of God's love for his people. For through baptism, *all of us* are missionaries of the Good News, since the Church is missionary by her very nature.

Silence is golden

'The Lord is in his holy Temple: let the whole earth be silent before him' (Habakkuk 2:20). In order to hear God speaking to us we need silence. A key element of the Knock apparition was its silent nature; neither the Lamb, nor Mary, nor Joseph nor John the Apostle say one word (even though the Evangelist appears to be preaching), yet this silence speaks volumes! Silence – not just an absence of words, but a loving desire to adore the Lamb – begets a joyful expectancy that God will speak to us. Within silence, we encounter the presence of the one who is Love, we can experience a glimpse of heaven: 'there was silence in heaven for about half an hour' (Revelation 8:1).

The terrible poverty of much of nineteenth-century Ireland – particularly in the West – and the great famine of the late 1840s, which left its mark on the land and its people for decades, is the inescapable backdrop to the event of 1879 in Knock. Certainly, if the Lord chose this quiet spot in the West to reveal his loving word in the silence of the heavenly vision, it was principally to bring a glimmer of hope to a broken people, and to stir up their faith in him. Today, however, there is another kind of hunger: 'See what days are coming – it is the Lord who speaks – days when I will bring famine on the country, a famine not of bread, a drought not of water, but of hearing the word of the Lord' (Amos 8:11). In our world today, while many suffer material poverty, how many more are starving for the word of the Lord, since his word has been drowned by the noise that surrounds us.

The Mother who saw the need of newly-weds at Cana now comes to us, to help us to make a space for her Son's word in our hearts, and to do whatever he tells us (cf. John 2:3–4). A mother always wants the best food for her children; in Knock Mary stands imploring heaven, winning for us by her powerful intercession the food of

God's Word, the food of the Bread of Life in the Eucharist, and a desire to say yes to God's loving plans for us. 'My food is to do the will of him who sent me, and to complete his work,' says Jesus (John 4:34). When we strive to do God's will, we find a taste for heaven on earth; when we contemplate the Lamb of Knock, surrounded by angels, we are drawn to become a little more of what we are called to be.

An invitation

We could describe the Knock phenomenon as a *divine secret*. In its biblical sense, a secret (or mystery) is something that is incomprehensible to us human beings without a special light from God. The secret of the Knock apparition, this vision without words, is awesome in its depth and radiance: as we'll discover, it reveals the Trinity, the mysteries of our redemption, the sacraments and, above all, the beauty and splendour of Jesus the Lamb of God, our Bread from heaven, the one who gives himself completely to us, and invites us to give ourselves to him, in a covenant relationship of mutual sacrificial love.

So whether or not you are already one of the many friends of Knock, whether you live near or far, or are simply curious, let's go in spirit to the Apparition Chapel, to contemplate the beautiful sculptures that represent what those witnesses saw on 21 August 1879, to learn something of what the Lord is telling us today, on our own path to the kingdom.

The fruit of silence is prayer.
The fruit of prayer is faith.
The fruit of faith is love.
The fruit of love is service.
The fruit of service is peace.

St Teresa of Calcutta

Joseph
Icon of the Father

This, then, is what I pray, kneeling before the Father, from whom every family, whether spiritual or natural, takes its name: out of his infinite glory, may he give you the power through his Spirit for your hidden self to grow strong, so that Christ may live in your hearts through faith, and then, planted on love and built on love, you will with all the saints have strength to grasp the breadth and the length, the height and the depth; until, knowing the love of Christ, which is beyond all knowledge, you are filled with the utter fullness of God.

Ephesians 3:14–19

As we contemplate the vision in white marble with the Lamb at the centre, something strikes us: of the three persons on the left hand side, St Joseph is the only one turned toward the Lamb! His posture is one of veneration, even adoration, head bowed and hands clasped in reverence. Joseph the carpenter is the original Quiet Man; no words of his can be found in the Gospel, yet his role as Mary's husband and protector, and foster-father to our Lord himself, gives him a unique place in salvation history. Think about it: the man who had the responsibility of caring for the Incarnate Word and the Immaculate Conception must have been made of tough stuff!

Merciful like the Father

Joseph was indeed tough, but in the sense of strong, or reliant; his combined qualities of gentleness and strength, dependability and hard-working vigour, all of which radiate from so many holy pictures of him over the centuries, can be summed up in one word: fatherly. And Joseph will be asked by the angel to *name* this child to be born of Mary; 'you must name him Jesus, because he is the one who is to save his people from their sins' (Matthew 1:21). Names were important for the Jews, they expressed identity. *Yeshua*, the name of Jesus in Hebrew, means 'the Lord saves', and even implies the sacred Name of the Lord; we could translate it as 'I am the one who saves'. The very being of Jesus is for us and for our salvation.

God wanted a father-figure to be there for his incarnate Son; yes, Jesus is divine, but he is also human: as a boy growing up, he needs a dad to help him mature, humanly speaking. So we can deduce that Joseph must be a true father, indeed an *icon of the Father* – so much needed in our times.

When Pope Francis declared the recent Year of Mercy (2015–16), the watchword he chose to accompany this special year of grace was, 'Merciful like the Father' – this comes from Luke's Gospel (6:36), though the exact wording appears more clearly in other languages like Italian: 'Be merciful (or compassionate) as your Father is merciful.' If the Holy Spirit inspired the Pope to call a special year dedicated to God's mercy, surely its purpose was to bring us to a greater understanding of the nature of God's fatherhood, for he is our origin and our final goal.

For many, the word 'father' has negative connotations; how many deep wounds exist in families, how many have suffered from father figures, or others in authority? God knows this. He came to reveal what a true father is; human parents, however much they try, can never perfectly reflect God's love and kindness. So God sent his Son, to show us in a human face what he is like. When Jesus says to his closest friends, 'Whoever sees me sees the Father,' it is in response to Philip's request, 'Let us see the Father and then we shall be satisfied' (John 14:8–9). *Let us see the Father*: this sums up our deep-rooted desire, the most profound yearning of all human flesh, to set eyes on the One who made us (cf. Psalms 99:3), who thought of us and chose us before the foundation of the world (cf. Ephesians 1:4), and who longs for us to be with him in perfect joy for ever: 'he brought us to life with Christ – it is through grace that you have been saved – and raised us up with him and gave us a place with him in heaven, in Christ Jesus' (Ephesians 2:5–6).

A young atheist friend, who was always emphatically seeking to affirm the non-existence of any god or creator, let the cat out of the bag one day when she blurted out, 'Ok, I do believe God exists, I'm just angry with him!' One might suspect that many self-declared atheists carry this anger toward God around with them, resulting from past hurts; we can pray that his tender love would heal them and bring them to know him as he really is. If we experience anger with regard to God, if he sometimes seems remote, or too 'all-other', almighty yet inaccessible, we could go and sit with St Joseph for a while. He can help us to encounter the real Father – not the one we might have made an imperfect image of, the one onto whom we project our own ancestral wounds – but the true Creator of our being and of the whole cosmos, who didn't just make us in his own image and likeness, but calls us, through grace, to be his own children! When we look to Joseph, we see something of what we want to be, deep down: for he is profoundly caring and protective, always there for his children who ask his intercession, the guardian who defends us from evil and who will never let us down. The opening passages of Matthew's Gospel portray a man of honour who wants to do the right thing, who seeks to spare Mary negative publicity at a time of possible scandal, a man who listens to the Lord speaking to him in dreams through his angel, his messenger (Matthew 1–2). We observe the total harmony between God's instructions and Joseph's simple obedience – which led to exile in Egypt, with all its trauma, in order to protect the divine Child from Herod who sought to kill him. If we asked Joseph what his secret is, how he managed to cope with such burdensome responsibility, he might answer with the words he heard from the angel of the Lord in his dream: 'Be not afraid to take Mary home' (Matthew 1:20). How could Joseph keep worrying, if Mary was there? She helped him to trust in the Lord, who never abandons those who turn to him. God always imparts his graces according to the particular tasks he asks of us, even if we don't always perceive it; having entrusted Joseph with a unique mission in world history, God would give him all the help he needed.

Obedience saves

When I hear the word 'obedience', I often think of my American friend Fr Tom Showalter (1957–2013), who was in my class in Rome. In the summer of 1996, Tom asked permission to fly back early to Europe, to attend my priestly ordination in France; this was initially granted, and he reserved a flight. However, as he explained to me in a letter, his superior had changed his mind, asking Tom to stay and work in the States before returning to Rome. He was a bit fed up, but wrote 'obedience, boy', and cancelled his ticket. The very plane he'd booked his seat on tragically crashed – there were no survivors. Tom, who became a priest the following year, often prayed for the person who took his place. After fruitful missions in Russia and the US, he died some years ago of heart failure and is missed by many. Given the great devotion Tom had to St Joseph, he would agree with him that obedience to God's will is life-saving!

Take Mary home

The Knock apparition reminds us of what we could call the 'Marian inclusion' of the four Gospels: in the very first chapter of the first Gospel, the angel commands Joseph to take Mary home; then, near the end of the fourth Gospel, Jesus entrusts her to John, the beloved disciple, who 'made a place for her in his home' (John 19:27). It's as if the whole Gospel is wrapped in Mary's mantle; if we want to find the key to the Gospel message, we could do worse than begin by taking Mary home, into our lives. As she stands in Knock between Joseph and John, she invites us to trust, as she surely helped Joseph himself to trust, and we will discover that God's grace is never lacking to empower us for the particular tasks given to us by God's loving plan.

We mustn't forget a special feature of the Knock vision: it presents a married couple! The heavenly messengers seem to appear together, in order to encourage those committed to each other by the sacramental bond of matrimony to be faithful, knowing that God will be with them. If, as at the wedding feast of Cana (John 2:1–12), the wine of human love may eventually run short, the divine Bridegroom can transform the water of our poverty into the wine of abundance, if we ask him through the intercession of Mary and Joseph. Also, Joseph, who adopted Jesus as his own son, can help those who are adopted, and their adoptive parents, to grow in his love, and to find healing from past wounds – and remind all of us that we are called to be God's adopted children, through his pure gift.

Men becoming fathers

A particular joy for the priest is to witness his male friends becoming dads, to see them maturing and learning fatherhood 'on the job', you might say. As one new father told me after the birth of the first of his three sons, 'Now I understand what it means that God gave up his only Son – I wouldn't give up my son for anyone!' God teaches us through the school of daily life; through family circumstances, human relationships and the ups and downs of every life experience. He never stops speaking to us, helping us to grow and enter more fully into a loving relationship with him. This sheds light on – and brings healing for – our fragile human relationships. Therefore, whatever our hurts, setbacks and disappointments, we can at any moment welcome the mercy of the Father, who wants to forgive our mistakes, bind our wounds and restore hope for the future. We could even say that, for the Christian, there is no such thing as regret: if we believe that 'by turning everything to their good, God co-operates with all those who love him' (Romans 8:28), then we can trust that even our worst mistakes or most negative experiences, drowned in his compassion, have enabled him to bring us closer to him. May St Joseph help us to leave the past to God's mercy, the future to his Providence, and rest in the 'present' of his loving Presence.

God gave up his only Son: to grasp something of what this fatherhood means, we can read the account of Abraham's sacrifice (Genesis 22). Why would God ask Abraham to sacrifice his only son Isaac? We cannot fathom his ways, yet we can surmise that in a pagan culture in which child sacrifice was rife, God put Abraham to the test in order to redeem something of this culture, and to bring him a long way on a journey of faith. When Abraham heard Isaac's question to his father, it must have cut him to the heart: 'Here are the fire and the wood, but where is the lamb for the burnt offering?' Abraham's reply, at first glance seeking to allay his son's fears, becomes a prophecy: 'God himself will provide the lamb for the burnt offering' (Genesis 22:7–8). Of course, we know the happy ending to the story; the angel of the Lord interrupts Abraham at the moment of sacrifice, and provides a ram for the offering. But the re-reading of this passage in the liturgy, during the Easter Vigil, reminds us that God did indeed provide the Lamb for the sacrifice. 'Since God did not spare his own Son, but gave him up to benefit us all, we may be certain, after such a gift, that he will not refuse anything he can give' (Romans 8:32). We will never understand fully on this earth what it cost the Father to send his Son to die for us; the story of Abraham, and the silent faith witness of Joseph, help us to learn gratitude and to draw more deeply from this well of salvation that is the sacrifice of the Lamb. 'Through his wounds, you have been healed' (1 Peter 2:24).

Go to Joseph!

In the seminary I attended for some years, there was a large statue of St Joseph with the Latin inscription, *Ite ad Ioseph*

('Go to Joseph!') The citation is scriptural, but of course refers to another Joseph, from the Old Testament, during a time of famine in Egypt: 'Pharaoh told all the Egyptians, 'Go to Joseph and do what he tells you' (Genesis 41:55) – which finds an echo in Mary's words to the stewards at the wedding of Cana. The name Joseph means 'God adds' (or increases), implying blessing and fruitfulness; this is an appropriate description of the young Joseph, son of Jacob. Betrayed by his brothers and sold into slavery in Egypt, he becomes the saviour of his clan in time of famine. How often our Joseph must have pondered this ancient story during his time of exile in Egypt with Mary and the child Jesus! Did he suspect that this boy, entrusted to him, would be betrayed by his own people, yet that the very means of this betrayal would become the instrument of their deliverance? When we go to Joseph, God increases his blessings. Remember the widow who kept 'pestering' the unjust judge in the parable (Luke 18:5). Every parent knows what pestering means: they'd much rather have their children pestering them than not speaking to them at all. So Joseph is happy for us to keep pestering him for our loved ones; he can help parents to intercede for their children, while at the same time helping them to let go of them, teaching them how to be there for their offspring without being controlling. When we see the Father's kind gentleness reflected in this great saint, we are encouraged to overcome any regret for past mistakes or temptation to despair. Thereby when we encounter this mercy which is beyond anything we can ever understand, this gives us hope that even we can become merciful like the Father.

It's a long way to Tipperary

There are still a few old-timers living in Knock village today who knew the last of the witnesses to the 1879 apparition (who died in the 1930s and 1940s). This reminds us of the importance of oral history, of treasuring our links with generations past – as I realise whenever I meet someone from Tipperary who remembers the clothes store of my late grandmother's family in Thurles. When we read the genealogy of Jesus (in Matthew 1 and Luke 3) we savour God's plan unfolding slowly but inexorably through the human generations. In addition to St Joseph, the parents of Mary are also honoured in Knock: the church of Shanvaghera (the other church of Knock parish), built in 1936, is dedicated to St Anne, Our Lady's own mother, reminding us of the importance of grandparents and their place in society, in handing on faith and tradition. We see this 'handing on' throughout the history of the Church: St

Irenaeus of Lyons, who preached in the second century, told of how he used to listen to the elderly St Polycarp, who as a young man sat at the feet of St John the Apostle, hearing his insistent call for believers to love one another, a call he had received from the Master himself. 'His mercy is from generation to generation upon those who fear him' (Luke 1:50). When we go to St Joseph, we encounter a man of deep faith, and through him we meet a people, the humble of Israel who feared God and awaited a Saviour. 'Only faith can guarantee the blessings that we hope for, or prove the existence of the realities that at present remain unseen. It was for faith that our ancestors were commended' (Hebrews 11:1–2).

May Joseph help us to rediscover where we come from, and to find, deep down, who we are: God's beloved children, called to glory.

> St Joseph, chosen by God to be the husband of Mary,
> the protector of the Holy Family,
> the guardian of the Church,
> protect all families in their work and recreation
> and guard us on our journey through life.
>
> from the Knock Novena prayer (see Appendix)

JOHN
The Beloved Son

Near the cross of Jesus stood his mother and his mother's sister, Mary the wife of Cleopas, and Mary of Magdala. Seeing his mother and the disciple he loved standing near her, Jesus said to his mother, 'Woman, this is your son'. Then to the disciple he said, 'This is your mother'. And from that moment the disciple made a place for her in his home.

John 19:25–7

The Gospel now comes alive in a profound way: we see John, the disciple Jesus loved, standing there, beside the Cross, where the Lamb fulfils God's saving plan. The mission for which Jesus came into this world is now being accomplished, as he lays down his life for the nation – 'and not for the nation only, but to gather together in unity the scattered children of God' (John 11:52). At this key moment in human history, when God's own beloved Son offers his life for the entire human race – from our first parents to those living on earth at the end of time – only a handful of his followers are present: a few women, including of course his dear Mother, and just one of his apostles, the one he loved. In his hour of need, Jesus sees that most of his friends have run away; only this small group remain till the end. But John is there! (We're following the constant tradition of the Church Fathers of the early centuries, which held that John the Apostle, the writer of the fourth Gospel and the beloved disciple were all one and the same person – a view shared by many modern Scripture scholars.) John chooses not to name himself in his Gospel, depicting himself rather as *the disciple Jesus loved* – so if he is not named, this suggests that he stands there for each of us: every single one of us is the beloved disciple, a child of God redeemed by the blood of the Lamb, and destined for the happiness of the kingdom. Through Baptism, we have been adopted as God's beloved children: what Jesus is by nature – the only-begotten, the eternal Son of the Father – we are through grace: 'before the world was made, he chose us in Christ, to be holy and spotless, and to live through love in his presence' (Ephesians 1:4). John's silent witness here at the Cross, standing between the innocent Lamb and the Immaculate one, is for us. In all our crosses and struggles, we should never forget that we are God's beloved children, that we have been washed in the blood of the Saviour. 'Nothing can ever come between us and the love of God made visible in Christ Jesus our Lord' (Romans 8:39).

How did they know it was John?

Pilgrims contemplating the Knock apparition as depicted in the dazzling white statues of the Shrine Chapel must often wonder: how did they know it was St John the Apostle? Mary and Joseph seem fairly easy to identify, but why John? Reading the witnesses' accounts as they testified to the original commission of 1879, we are struck by how simply, almost spontaneously, they identified the mitred figure as John; for some, it very much resembled a statue of this saint (without a mitre) that was in the nearby chapel of Lecanvey, near Westport. Taking the 'holy instinct' of the witnesses together with John's account of the Lord's Passion in his Gospel, it rings true; surely, no one else could possibly stand between the crucified Lamb and his blessed Mother apart from the disciple who stood by the Cross, destined to record for all time those saving events in his Gospel.

Beloved disciple of the Lord

Yes, John is a 'faithful priest' and 'teacher of the Word of God', the great apostle and evangelist, to whom the heavens were torn open anew during his exile at Patmos, when he wrote his Apocalypse ('Unveiling' or Revelation), the last book of the Bible. However, John is, first and formost, the disciple Jesus loved; this is the starting point for us, as we learn to become what we are, God's dear children.

Of course, Jesus loves everyone equally; he doesn't have favourites, as we would understand the term! Nevertheless, he does have close friends: we often see him take Peter, James and John aside to be with him at certain moments in his public life. Jesus came to tell us we were loved by the Father, all of us, infinitely; but the more we respond to his love, the more he can fill us with his manifold gifts. 'As the Father has loved me, so I have loved you. Remain in my love' (John 15:9). We can suspect that John responded to his invitation wholeheartedly, even more than the other disciples; yet John's message to us is that each of us can encounter this love, become friends of Jesus and – in a certain way – *become Jesus*, because when the Father looks upon us, he sees the image of his eternal Son in us!

'God is love' (1 John 4:8, 16): in the Trinity, from all eternity to all eternity, the Father loves the Son, the Son returns the Father's perfect love, and the love between them is so infinitely great that it is a person, the Holy Spirit. God has no need of anything outside himself, he wasn't compelled to create the stars or the planets, the angelic or human realms. Yet, he wanted to share his love: he willed to create beings with free will who could choose to return his love. He designed us with the capacity to know him, to choose to love him, and even to 'share the divine nature' (2 Peter 1:4) – this gives each of us an awesome dignity, that can never be taken from us! Therefore, because we are made in his *image* (what we are) and *likeness* (what we will be), this challenges us to look upon ourselves and others in a new light. This calls us to respect each person since each person has been created uniquely, called by God's plan to something very great and beautiful: 'in so far as you did this to one of the least of these brothers of mine, you did it to me' (Matthew 25:40).

So when Jesus came to this earth, he didn't simply tell us God loved us, with a nice smile (though Jesus surely had a wonderful smile!) – he lived each moment, to its utmost, as the Father's beloved Son, to show us how to live each moment of our lives. Through thick and thin, in joy or in sorrow, at work or at rest, if we could decide to live each day as a beloved son or daughter of the Father, what a witness to the world this would be! Furthermore, when we contemplate John, there by the Cross, we see a son of God who knows he's loved, and who is given a special mission to proclaim this love, this dignity of sonship, by his preaching and his writing. The witnesses to the apparition were insistent that John was preaching (though silently) with book in hand and arm raised; what else could he be saying other than repeating the Lord's words in his Gospel: 'Do not let your hearts be troubled' … 'Love one another, as I have loved you' … 'Be brave, I have conquered the world!' (John 14:1; 15:12; 16:33).

Behold your Mother!

It is the hour of darkness, of apparent defeat; the one who is Life is put to death, he who came to bring peace and freedom is cruelly tortured and executed by wicked men. The Cross is the ultimate paradox of human existence: the all-powerful one accepts being pinned to the wood of a tree, for us and for our salvation; the life-giver welcomes his own death, in order to bring us life. He who 'went about doing good and curing all who had fallen into the power of the devil' (Acts 10:38) is now the victim of the forces of evil. Does this mean that the evil one has the last word? No, it is precisely now, when Jesus can do no more, humanly speaking – he can no longer walk around, healing and delivering, those hands which blessed and liberated are now fixed to the Cross, he who is the Word of life can barely speak – that he completes the greatest work of his life on earth, the greatest act of love in human history: he saves us, by his death we have life, and evil is overcome by the Lamb who conquers! 'When I am lifted up from the earth, I shall draw all things to myself' (John 12:32).

Scholars tell us that John's Gospel emphasises, more than the others, that the Cross of the Lord is his *glory*, that the way of the Cross is the total glorification of the God made man, revealing the Father's love for humanity in the fullest way possible. 'Now has the Son of man been glorified, and in him God has been glorified' (John 13:31). This is so hard for us to grasp; how can the symbol of utter defeat be a sign of glory?

We have to stop there with John, with Mother Mary, asking them to shed light on our situation, our need. Through a special grace, John *stayed*; when all the Lord's other friends ran away, he remained there, in the darkness – so we can implore him to be there with us in our times of darkness, helping us to find hope, and so anticipate the new light of dawn. We now see completed the Gospel 'inclusion' mentioned in the previous chapter: just as Joseph took Mary home, and so welcomed *Yeshua*, the Lord who saves, now John receives the final precious gift from his Lord, welcoming Jesus' own Mother as his Mother; he 'made a place for her in his home'. We could say that *Joseph learned from Mary how to become a father, and John learned from her how to become a son.*

How could John remain there beholding such a heart-rending sight, his dear Master and best friend being crucified? How could he not run away? Because *she* was there: Mary stands by the Cross, she knows that the hour promised by her Son at Cana has come, that apparent darkness is destroyed by the Light of the world: 'the light that shines in the dark, the light that darkness could not overpower' (John 1:5). Mary had always believed in her Son; she had heard the promises of the angel, yet now her faith is tested to the utmost. 'Blessed is she who believed that the promise made her by the Lord would be fulfilled' (Luke 1:45).

Faith is a kind of *knowledge*, a light in the dark; hope is an *awaiting*, an expectation of what is believed in but not yet possessed. At the Cross, Mary believes; she may not understand how God will act, but she knows that death is not the end. She hopes against hope, waiting for the dawn that follows darkest day. Faith enables us to see beyond appearances; it helped Mother Teresa to see Jesus in the poorest of the poor, his 'distressing disguises'; [Faith] enabled St John Vianney to spend up to sixteen hours each day hearing confessions in his small parish church in Ars, for he knew this sacrament brought God's forgiveness and mercy to a great number of people in the most powerful and personal way. Faith empowers us to see the risen, glorified Body of our Lord in the Eucharist, in what appears to be flat, white bread. Faith enabled Mary, at the Cross, to see the glorification of her only child, her firstborn, while all appearances would indicate the utter contrary. 'If you believe, you will see the glory of God' (John 11:40).

Grief affects each of us in a unique way; none of us can predict in advance how we will react to the loss of a loved one, whether it occurs suddenly or after a long illness. At the Cross, each friend of Jesus lives through this darkest hour in their own way: Mary, John, Mary Magdalene and the other women, each of them has a private sanctuary of sorrow and pain which we can barely begin to understand, even less embrace. However, Mary's way of the Cross is singular in its intensity; she suffers more than the others, because she loves more. We could say that in her ardent desire to offer herself with the Lamb, for the salvation of the world, her immaculate heart is thrown wide open. She embodies in her very flesh every saving word of her Son, for she is Mother of the Word, Mother of Life. She can even make her own the testimony that Jesus declared before Pilate: 'I was born for this, I came into the world for this: to bear witness to the truth; and all who are on the side of truth listen to my voice' (John 18:37). Mary knows she was born for this moment too; her whole life finds its meaning at the Cross, which is the central event of human history. Her manner of living through this hour of sorrow helps John and the other women to stand there, in faith and hope. Her whole attitude speaks of one who still believes in the angel's promise, and who finds her blessing there. And she receives a final, parting gift from her crucified Child, in a way his last will and testament: 'Behold your son!' (John 19:26)

Mary surely understands what Jesus is doing: he is entrusting her to the beloved disciple, and through John to every disciple that he loves, so that she can be Mother of John, Mother of the Church, Mother of each one of us. Mary will now look at John with new eyes; in the mystical order, she has given birth to a new son, and the pain of Calvary will give way to the joy of the first Sunday. 'When she has given birth to the child she forgets the suffering, in her joy that a man has been born into the world' (John 16:21). Our Blessed Lady will be there with John, the Apostle of love, to help him live as the Father's beloved child; she is present, quietly and gently, by the Cross of each of us, her children, helping us to stand in faith, to await in hope and to grow in love, as she did. As believers, we know (at least in theory) that God brings good out of evil; the greatest sin ever committed – putting to death the very Son of God, sent to save us – is transformed into the greatest work of God's goodness, as the gates of heaven are opened wide for the whole human race. So Mary and John experience in faith what St Paul will later put into words: 'I think that what we suffer in this life can never be compared to the glory, as yet unrevealed, which is waiting for us' (Romans 8:18). It seems that those who have suffered much, yet who have found acceptance and peace, have had something of this blessedness revealed to them; we can all think of people we know who have been through trials we could scarcely imagine, and have 'come through to the other side', thus witnessing powerfully to the glory of God, the ocean of joy which drowns all sorrows, on that day when 'he will wipe away all tears from their eyes' (Apocalypse 21:4).

High Priest

Through his incarnation, Jesus is the High Priest: he is the bridge between heaven and earth, the one mediator between God and the human race (1 Timothy 2:5). The gap between the finger of God and that of Adam depicted so powerfully in Michelangelo's creation tableau is now breached; by embracing our human nature, he brings God and man together because he is both God and man. Jesus prays to the Father for us; he intercedes for his friends, and for those who are not yet his friends. In his priestly heart, he gathers up all the prayers and tears, the joys and sorrows of his Body the Church, to present them to the Father as an offering pleasing to him. In return, he receives from the

Father's hand the graces and blessings his children need, bestowed on each of them as his providence and loving plan decide.

But everything the Word made flesh possesses in himself is for us as his free gift! Through Baptism, every Christian shares in Christ's threefold mission as *priest*, *prophet* and *king* – as the Church reminds us through the anointing of chrism oil immediately after Baptism, even the tiniest baby and every one of us is a partaker of his triple mission: *priest* – called to intercede for the world, particularly through the sacraments; *prophet* – mandated to proclaim God's saving Word; and *king* – sent to be a steward of creation and guardian of the community of Christ's flock in charity. This isn't just a concept or a nice idea, it's the reality of what we are all called to live, in order to bring God's amazing grace into the world, and, by his mercy, to bring us – and a multitude of brothers and sisters – to eternal glory! All of us are called to be collaborators, co-workers with God (1 Corinthians 3:9), we could even say *co-mediators* between God and the human race, but always through him, with him and in him – Jesus, the one mediator.

The Second Vatican Council (1962–5) brought out, in a profound way, the common priesthood of all the baptised, while at the same time affirming the specific mission of the bishop and priest as teacher of the Word, minister of the sacraments and guardian of the community. The prayer to St John in the Knock Novena prayer brings together these three dimensions in a wonderfully succinct way: 'Help us to hunger for the Word, to be loyal to the Mass, and to love one another.'

'You did not choose me, no, I chose you,' says Jesus to his disciples at the Last Supper (John 15:16). So how did Jesus select Peter, John and the rest of the Twelve? 'I call you friends' (John 15:15) – this appears to be his main criterion for choosing his apostles, his first bishops, before considering their qualities of administration or preaching ability. His 'entrance examination' to aspiring disciples could be summed up in one simple statement, his question to Peter: 'Do you love me?' (John 21:15). As a cardinal tellingly said before entering into the 2013 conclave that elected Pope Francis, 'We're looking for a man like Peter, a man who loves Jesus more than the others!'

Yes, Peter denied his Master three times before a charcoal fire (John 18:18) but was reinstated by the Lord's mercy with his threefold query, 'Do you love me?' before a charcoal fire on the lakeside, after the Resurrection (John 21:9) – possibly Peter recalled the vision of Isaiah in the Temple, his sense of his own unworthiness healed by the seraph touching his mouth with live charcoal (Isaiah 6:5–7). In any case, Peter surely drew strength from John's presence; John will not blame Peter for denying his Lord and running away because John knows Peter's impulsive love for Jesus and his flock. Peter will accept the Lord's mercy and affirmation of his mission as chief shepherd; his awareness of his own weakness, stamped right through the Gospels, enables him to be a gentle and merciful leader in his turn.

How we'd have loved to have been present at a Mass celebrated by one of the apostles! They had received the mandate directly from our Lord at the Last Supper, 'Do this as a memorial of me' (Luke 22:19) – where 'memorial' or remembrance is more than just calling to mind, it implies re-living the event, rendering present the Lord's saving actions from the past. John's celebration of Mass, in particular, would have struck us deeply: as the beloved disciple who rested his head on the Master's breast, who witnessed the Cross and took Mary into his home, his words and sacred gestures must have made Christ present again to his people, in a most profound way.

His presence at Knock reminds us: every Mass accords us this grace! At every eucharistic celebration, heaven comes to meet earth. The angels are there, our Mother

Mary, the apostles and all the saints and our loved ones who are in heaven interceding for us. We hear the Word of life, then partake of Christ's loving sacrifice and receive his very Body and Blood; whatever the merits or particular gifts of the celebrant, however grandiose or humble the church or chapel, whether we are two or three gathered or two million (at World Youth Day celebrations, for example), it's the same Mass! It was a great blessing for me, not long after my ordination, to concelebrate morning Mass with a group around St John Paul II in his private chapel in Rome – but what struck me, apart from the intense prayer of this great Pope, was the simplicity of the liturgy; one could have been in a small country chapel with any pastor. This was a reminder that every Mass is special; every liturgical celebration of the faithful gathered together in love and truth is blessed by the Lord. But again, we need 'extras', that's why St John is there at Knock.

Unity in the work of service

So John, having learned from the Lord and his Mother to live as a son of God, can become a father, the ardent priest and apostle he is chosen to be, sent to proclaim the Lamb's victory of love; his journey will lead (tradition tells us) to Ephesus, then to exile on the island of Patmos, where he receives the visions that inspire the book of Revelation. However, we can also think of John's place in Knock as a sign for our priests of today, who visit the Shrine in great numbers. This great apostle of love speaks intimately to all priests, bringing them back in spirit to their original encounter with the Lord, their first call. John shines as a beacon of hope for the priest, encouraging him to come and rest his weary heart upon the Heart of the Lamb, and to welcome Mary anew into his life and ministry. If the sins of the few in Ireland and elsewhere have brought hurt and discouragement to many priests, as well as to the faithful and the wider community, John the beloved disciple helps us to find healing and regain courage; he enables us to go back to the fountain of our ministry, Jesus himself, who unceasingly tells us, 'I call you friends, because I have made known to you everything I have learnt from my Father' (John 15:15). Knock reminds us how many of the faithful pray for priests, and value their service; this awakens a spirit of thanksgiving and gratitude in us priests, and impels us to pray and work for the flock, for the common good, 'so that the saints together make a unity in the work of service, building up the body of Christ' (Ephesians 4:12). We all need each other. John's example shows us that if we all strive to live as God's beloved children, gazing with one heart and soul in adoration of the Lamb, with the Mother of Mercy at our side, we will gradually learn to become merciful like the Father, and paths to renewal will open up.

Finally, in chapter seventeen of John's Gospel, in what is called the priestly prayer of Christ, we find the high point of the Lord's relationship as Son with his heavenly Father, and in a certain way, the summit of the holy writings, opening up eternity to his friends whom he has chosen. 'Eternal life is this: to know you, the only true God, and Jesus Christ whom you have sent' (17:3). We'd like to know *how* John came to write down this intimate discourse; Scripture does not reveal all its secrets, but does reveal the mind of the Saviour, whose burning desire is to accomplish the Father's work, to pray for the ones he has chosen, and indeed 'for those also who through their words will believe in me' (John 17:20) – right up to us today, and unto the end of the ages. John would remind us of the Lord's urgent prayer, 'May they all be one, Father, may they be one in us, as you are in me and I am in you, so that the world may believe it was you who sent me' (17:21). Unity is not an option: it is the hallmark of the believing community, reflecting the perfect unity at the heart of the Trinity, in love and truth and beauty. Unity, however, is also a gift we can implore, asking the Lord to unveil the eyes of our minds to see what is lacking in our own selves in this regard. The final verse (17:26) seems to sum up the whole Gospel, and holds us in its embrace, so that we become part of sacred history: 'I have made you name known to them and will continue to make it known, so that the love with which you loved me may be in them, and so that I may be in them.'

St John, beloved disciple of the Lord,
faithful priest,
teacher of the Word of God,
help us to hunger for the Word,
to be loyal to the Mass,
and to love one another.

from the Knock Novena prayer (see Appendix)

MARY
Bride of the Spirit

The Spirit and the Bride say, 'Come'. Let all who are thirsty come: all who want it may have the water of life.

Apocalypse 22:17

She is there! When we look upon the Knock Apparition, our gaze is inevitably drawn to the Lady standing between St Joseph and St John, crowned, with hands outstretched, eyes raised to the sky in prayerful contemplation. Local tradition has ensured that whatever depth of meaning is encapsulated in the Knock message, it will forever be *Our Lady's Shrine*, and the long-standing devotion of the Irish to the Rosary, meditating the Gospel with Mary, surely drew her to appear in this spot where she was already loved and welcomed. Mary has an essential place in the Gospel story, as we have already gleaned; without her, there would be no Saviour: 'When the appointed time came, God sent his Son, born of a woman, born a subject of the Law, to redeem the subjects of the Law and to enable us to be adopted as sons' (Galatians 4:4). God could have chosen other ways to save us, but he chose to be 'born of a woman', and this required Mary's freely given 'yes'. That's fine, we might say, but it must have been easy for Mary to say yes; wasn't she the Immaculate Conception, predestined to be Mother of God? Indeed, however, Mary had free will just like us, she was free to say no, yet in her we see a wonderful cooperation between divine grace and human freedom. In a way, it was easy for Mary to say yes – because every choice she had made up to this point had already been a joyful yes to God's will.

Wherever there are people who do God's will, there is heaven, as Pope Benedict wrote in his commentary of the Lord's Prayer in *Jesus of Nazareth*. God had prepared a heaven for his Son's beginnings on earth, the Immaculate Heart of this quiet, gentle young woman of Nazareth. I'm told that in Japanese, the characters used to depict the maternal womb translate as 'temple of the child'; Mary, who went to the Temple in Jerusalem as a small child to offer herself fully to God, is now the true temple of the living God, the temple of the divine Child, a holy tabernacle from which the Saviour of all nations will be born.

In the light of the Knock tableau, we can read the scriptural passages describing three key events in salvation history – the Annunciation, Calvary and Pentecost: we find Mary there each time, and we find the Holy Spirit at work. St Maximilian Kolbe, following St Francis of Assisi, called Mary the 'Bride of the Holy Spirit', to express something of the deep union between God's eternal Spirit and his beloved creature. Saint Maximilian also daringly described Mary as a kind of incarnation of the Holy Spirit; this sort of expression causes theologians to go pale! Probably, what St Maximilian meant was that if the Holy Spirit did become human, he would resemble Mary more than anyone else – as she was the only human creature who perfectly fulfilled God's plans for her on this earth. When we look to her, the Immaculate, we are brought back to our *origin* – where we came from – since we glimpse the Lord's primordial plan for our nature, before sin ever was; and we anticipate our *destiny* – where we are going – because she shines out for us from heaven, where she is in glory, body and soul, as a foretaste and promise of what we shall be, if we strive to be faithful to the one who wills only our good.

The Annunciation
'In the sixth month the angel Gabriel was sent' (Luke 1:26): this event, portrayed in so many works of art through the centuries, is truly an encounter – a meeting between God's messenger and the young virgin of Nazareth. 'Rejoice, so highly favoured! The Lord is with you' (1:28). It is time to rejoice, because salvation is at hand; the Redeemer awaited by his people is to be born, born of you who are full of grace! Mary, a true daughter of Israel, knows the messianic prophecies: when she hears the angel's request, and the

promises about this child (1:32–3), there can be no doubt what she is being asked. This son of hers will be great, Son of the Most High; he will receive David's kingdom to rule over the house of Jacob for ever, and his reign will have no end – this can only be the Messiah predicted by the prophets centuries ago, the Holy One of God. How can this come about? 'The Holy Spirit will come upon you, and the power of the Most High will cover you with its shadow' (1:35); just as the glory of the Lord 'overshadowed' the Tabernacle during the Israelites' journey through the desert (Exodus 40:34–5), so the Holy Spirit will make of Mary his Bride, in order to bring to birth Jesus, the one who saves.

'I am the handmaid of the Lord' (1:38): Mary already lives and moves in the Spirit; the Spirit who is at work throughout Israel's history guides her every thought and action – but now, when the Lord receives her *Yes*, her complete availability to his plan, the Spirit will be as it were wedded to Mary's soul, in an utterly new way, to bring about the miracle of the virginal conception of Christ.

'Nothing is impossible to God' (1:37) – Gabriel's affirmation concerns the unhoped-for pregnancy of Mary's older cousin Elizabeth, to whom she will hasten without delay, inspired by the Spirit. And we know what happens next (Luke 1:39–41): when Mary simply says 'hello', little John the Baptist leaps in his mother's womb and Elizabeth is filled with the same Holy Spirit. Mary's simple greeting unleashes a powerful action of the Spirit! We see how profoundly the Spirit can work, once he finds a willing soul that wholeheartedly embraces his presence. The Visitation also reminds us of the spiritual capacity of the unborn child, which impels us to pray and work for the protection of every human life, from its very beginnings; as a car-sticker once put it so simply, 'Your Mom was pro-life.'

Nothing is impossible to God: this is surely what Mary wants to remind us now, as we come to her feet burdened by so many worries and cares. She stands there inviting us to grow in trust in her Lord, who has worked great things for her and through her; above all, she wants us to welcome the Spirit, 'whom God has given to those who obey him' (Acts 5:32). Many of us recite the Angelus each day, repeating Mary's yes: 'Behold the handmaid of the Lord'; we also say 'Thy will be done' each time we pray the Our Father. God takes all our prayers to heart; if we really mean what we say, if we seek his will and welcome him with all our hearts, as Mary did, we will experience the power of the Spirit, and there will be 'sacred spaces' throughout our land, where heaven's presence is felt. We might feel this is all just for the great saints, but Mary wants each one of us to discover the joy of saying yes to God's loving will, for she knows that there is nothing impossible to him.

Calvary

Mary is there at the Cross, in faith and hope, as she joins her offering to that of the Lamb: she is truly the *Woman of the Eucharist*, who stands between heaven and earth, inviting us to adore her Son, as he gives his life for the world. As she witnesses her Lord's sacrifice, she receives the gift of a new son in John, the beloved disciple. But also, she knows that Jesus must return to the Father, in order to send us his Spirit. He had made it clear to his friends at the Last Supper: 'It is for your own good that I am going because unless I go, the Advocate will not come to you' (John 16:7), the Advocate being the Spirit who comes to console and strengthen those who follow Jesus. And now at the consummation of his supreme sacrifice, the Lord says his last words, 'I am thirsty' (John 19:28) – the terrible physical thirst caused by the loss of so much blood, but also an expression of his loving thirst for us, and his desire to give living water – the Holy Spirit – to those who believe in him. Mary, already filled with the Spirit, joins her thirst to his; she brings all her children, those who thirst for life and truth, and those who don't yet know their thirst, in spirit to Calvary. 'If you only knew what God is offering,' Jesus had said to the Samaritan woman at the well, 'you would have been the one to ask, and he would have given you living water' (John 4:10). If we only knew the gift of God, we wouldn't waste so much time on less important things. But God is good, and he sends us his Mother, to help us to look up, to behold the one we have pierced by our sins (cf. Zachariah 12:10 and John 19:37), and to find mercy and peace. 'It is accomplished' are Christ's final words in John's Gospel (19:30) – our redemption is won for us, heaven is rendered accessible to poor sinners, and a new world is created. The evangelist then concludes the same verse: 'bowing his head he gave up his spirit.'

Did John understand this to mean that the Lord's death enabled the Spirit to be given? Many experts think so. As he returns to the Father, Jesus can now send the Advocate to his friends who grieve for him; his death is not the end, but a new beginning. He brings our human nature to a new dignity and greatness, and despite her sorrow Mary is at peace, for the hour of darkness will be followed by the hour of the Spirit, the joy of the Resurrection.

We can see echoes of this action of the Spirit at times of grief: when a holy person leaves this earth, there is new grace and strength for those left behind. The very public death and funeral of St John Paul II in 2005 showed this in a spectacular, global way, but there are many other, more hidden examples of how the Holy Spirit works when a good person dies in grace. They go to the Father, following the way that Jesus showed us by his own death, and the Spirit is imparted for the benefit of many, especially for those they loved on this earth. Mary accompanies this final journey, renewing her loving *Fiat*, her yes, on behalf of all her children, living and dead. We can make ours the words of Fr Lingard's hymn: 'Refuge in grief, star of the sea, pray for the mourner, pray for me.'

Pentecost

The Spirit has already been given, but now he must fill his friends in a completely new way, in order to send them out to the ends of the earth, to bring everyone to know the Good News of this new life. After his Resurrection, Jesus has ascended to the Father; once more, he returns to the Father's house, now glorified and raised to new life by the power of the Spirit. The apostles have to wait in prayer for nine days – the first *novena* in Church history, and the template for every novena; they are gathered in the Upper Room 'in continuous prayer, together with several women, including Mary the mother of Jesus' (Acts 1:14).

Jesus didn't leave a guidebook explaining how to start the Church; he sent his Spirit! The apostles had met the Risen One, they were filled with joy, but what would happen next? They didn't know what was going on – however, Mary was with them. She who was already overshadowed by the power of the Most High prayed with that small, fearful group of men – together with several women, a vital feature of this nascent Church, whose presence surely helped these men to pray and to trust. When we pray without knowing what God is up to, when we hang on in there, praying and waiting with Mary, the Bride of the Spirit, then God can do what he wills. And his will is always good.

Pentecost was a Jewish feast, taking place fifty days after the Passover, when men would make a pilgrimage to Jerusalem to celebrate the first fruits of the harvest. Now it takes on a whole new meaning: a mighty wind from heaven – sign of the Spirit who blows where he will (cf. John 3:8) – fills the house in which the disciples were sitting, and tongues of fire rest on the head of each of them (cf. Acts 2:2–3) – for the Spirit, the fire of God's love, is one, yet manifold in his gifts. 'They were all filled with the Holy Spirit, and began to speak foreign languages' (2:4): the Spirit enables us to speak a new language, proclaiming his saving works in new ways. These weak, timid men are impelled to go out to the public squares, to those Jewish pilgrims that came from near and far, 'each one bewildered to hear these men speaking his own language' (2:5). The Spirit speaks our language; he meets each of us in our own cultural context. If we call on the Spirit, he can help us to speak to others in their own language, to find the right words which touch hearts and bring new hope.

In Knock Shrine, we must hope and believe that the Spirit is present. If Mary is there, arms raised to heaven, interceding for her apostles of today, surely the Spirit is given! The Shrine priests can witness how passers-by or casual tourists can become pilgrims, friends of the Lord: how many have taken the step of going to confession, often for the first time in years, while saying, 'I never even meant to come to Knock, I just found myself here'? Some years ago, an American friend on a journey with his mother stopped off in Knock (to use the rest room); his mother, a devout Southern Baptist 'who had probably never met a Catholic', he later told me, popped into the Apparition Chapel to say a prayer. 'Gee, the Holy Spirit is being poured out, you only have to sit there!' she exclaimed.

You only have to sit there: this is what pilgrims have been doing in Knock for decades; this is what the apostles did in the Upper Room, with the essential factor that Mary was there, and the Spirit came. And she is here, in her Shrine, welcoming all her children, wanting each one of them to experience the love, joy and peace that the Spirit brings (cf. Galatians 5:22).

It is wonderful for us to be here

We have seen how Mary was 'overshadowed' by the Spirit at the Lord's Annunciation. There is just one other place in the Gospels where the same word is used, at the *Transfiguration*: Jesus had taken Peter, James and John with him up the mountain, where 'he was transfigured' (Mark 9:2), in other words, his appearance was changed; he revealed his glory to his close friends, in anticipation of the risen state which he would enjoy after passing through death to new life. Moses and Elijah appeared on the mountain, talking with Jesus. Peter and his companions were overwhelmed, he merely blurted out, 'Rabbi, it is wonderful for us to be here' (9:5). And then 'a cloud came, covering them in shadow, and there came a voice from the cloud, "This is my Son, the Beloved. Listen to him"' (9:7). Like the Baptism of Jesus, this is an event where the Trinity is revealed: the Spirit is present in the cloud, 'overshadowing' the disciples, and the Father's voice is heard, while we behold the splendour of his divine Son.

The Transfiguration event was not strictly necessary but a Gospel 'extra' if you like; it has always been understood by the Church as helping to strengthen the faith of the disciples before the Lord must undergo his Passion. We could see the Knock Apparition as a kind of *transfiguration event*, a sign of hope to a people living through great trial, reminding them that heaven is with them, and exhorting them to gaze on the glory of the beloved Son and listen to him.

But why are Moses and Elijah there? Traditionally, they represent the Law and the Prophets of the Old Testament, now fulfilled in Christ. But we can go further: ever since creation, when God made all things through his *word* (Genesis 1) and his *breath* (Genesis 2), we see this 'double action' of God manifesting his power through his Word (Jesus) and his Spirit throughout Scripture. 'By his word the heavens were made, by the breath of his mouth all the stars' – 'He sends forth his word and it melts them: at the breath of his mouth the waters flow' (Psalm 32:6 and 147:18) and so on. By analogy, we can see Moses as giver of the Word (the Law) and Elijah the prophet in the Spirit – though of course Moses receives the Spirit too, and Elijah proclaims the word, the concepts are interchangeable. But this twofold creative action – echoed in

God's two witnesses of Apocalypse 10 – can help us find an ever-greater harmony in today's Church, the object of God's hierarchical and charismatic gifts.

In simple terms, the priest (represented by St John) must proclaim the Word and govern the community; but the People of God (represented by Mary) are bestowed with gifts of the Spirit, who can inspire all to grow in love and fidelity. The pastor has the authority to govern, yet must take into account the gifts and insights God gives to the faithful; this inevitably causes tension sometimes, but we are all called to 'listen to what the Spirit is saying to the churches' (Apocalypse 2:7 – incidentally, the Lord's command to the church in Ephesus, where John was probably its first bishop). When we come before Mary and John in Knock, they encourage all of us – pastors and people – to be open to the Spirit, so that God's message can spread more effectively.

Just as the Father asked of us on the mountain to listen to his beloved Son, Mary at the wedding feast of Cana reiterates this by saying, 'Do whatever he tells you' (John 2:5). If she can say this, it's because she knows we can hear his voice, which we will if we accept to be part of his flock – 'the sheep that belong to me listen to my voice,' says Jesus (John 10:27). She *magnifies* his words for us, so that we can hear more clearly what he is saying, and she also gives us every help in accomplishing what he asks of us. This brings us back to the meaning of silence; the apparition without words empowers us to hear God's Word and even to *become* a word of love and light from God, for others. 'You do not ask for sacrifice and offerings, but an open ear' (Psalm 39:7).

So as we sit close to Mary at her Shrine, we take heart in difficult times. Many are fearful for the future, seeing our poor world spiralling to godless destruction. Things may have to get worse before they get better; however, the Lamb will conquer (cf. Apocalypse 17:14), and as Mary promised at Fatima, 'In the end my Immaculate Heart will triumph.' So we gain courage, and we can truly say, like Peter on the mountain, it is wonderful for us to be here!

Mother and Queen

'Now a great sign appeared in heaven: a woman, adorned with the sun, standing on the moon, and with the twelve stars on her head for a crown' (Apocalypse 12:1).

Several of the witnesses to the Knock Apparition testified that the Blessed Virgin was wearing a crown, variously described as 'brilliant', 'rather large', 'of a golden brightness'. The crown not only symbolises royalty, or favour bestowed by God, but also the saints who have triumphed over sin and death, including in a special way martyrs, those who gave their lives for Christ (the Greek word for martyr has as its primary meaning 'witness'; also, the name of St Stephen, the first Christian martyr, comes from the Greek term for a crown). True, St Thérèse did describe Our Lady as being 'more mother than queen', but we can understand that she is Queen because she is Mother of the great King; rewarded for her great faith and humble service of her divine Son, she now reigns with him in glory.

Mary truly is our spiritual Mother who watches over our every need with loving tenderness and compassion for our weakness. She is also a powerful Queen, with might and authority delegated to her by her divine Son, able to work in our lives, removing obstacles on our path and 'untying the knots' which hamper us on our journey to the kingdom. Because she carried the Lord in her womb with so much love, and brought him up as any mother would bring up her child, yet with an intensity of maternal care never seen elsewhere, she can apply the same care to us, because she sees our need. She wants us so much to live as God's beloved children, and she has the means in hand to orient everything in our lives to this goal. Her manifest perfections and various titles might discourage us from drawing closer to her; but that's not what God wants. Sure, no modern parent is perfect; as I sometimes remind pilgrims, there was only one perfect wife and mother in history, and her statue is in the Shrine Chapel! But her royal beauty and immaculate goodness are our shining light, a sign of hope for us as we stumble along in this vale of tears, a promise of what we ourselves are called to be, and what we shall become one day with God's grace and her help, 'holy and immaculate before him in love' (Ephesians 1:4), in complete perfection of love and happiness, with the vast multitude of the saints, every one a new friend and companion, for ever.

They say it's good to have friends in high places – 'With God on our side, who can be against us?' (Romans 8:31) – and if God gives us Mary, St Joseph and St John to guide us, each one reflecting in a particular way the mystery of the Trinity, then we can be sure we'll have all the help we need.

As we now turn to the centrepiece of the Knock Apparition, the Lamb of God, we can give thanks. We begin to suspect that what was revealed in this small Mayo village many years ago is something far greater than we can grasp at first glance. All our efforts at penetrating the secret of Knock are mere scratchings at the surface – as with all

God's mysteries, there are ever more hidden depths to his message than we will ever discover in this world. But he is happy when we seek to understand more clearly what he is saying to us, and our every modest attempt to welcome his gift will be rewarded with blessings, multiplied like ripples of joy, spreading through our world.

We give thanks with Mary. Mary's song of praise, which bursts forth from her lips during her encounter with Elizabeth, is largely composed of passages from the Old Testament, the holy book of her people. However, Mary doesn't just string together some good Bible quotes! Inspired by the Spirit, she makes this canticle her own, praising God with words from his own Word. 'All generations will call me blessed', something unthinkable for a young Jewish woman to say, coming from a small town in the back of beyond, yet prophetic words fulfilled anew each time we recite a *Hail Mary*. She lauds God who raises up the poor and humble to royal dignity as children of the kingdom, while casting down the proud and mighty of this world.

Whenever we read or recite the *Magnificat* we can think of the Eucharist – as we recall, her canticle is proclaimed while she bears the Saviour in her womb, so she is our model of thanksgiving, particularly after Holy

Communion, when we welcome the Lord into our own bodies. As we contemplate the Lamb with her, we can be grateful, like Elizabeth, for God's goodness: 'Why should I be honoured with a visit from the mother of my Lord?' (Luke 1:43). At Knock, in a special way, but wherever we are, she visits us, to bring us Jesus, to set our hearts on fire with his love, imploring the Spirit to come as in a new Pentecost, for us and all God's children.

> My soul proclaims the greatness of the Lord
> and my spirit exults in God my saviour;
> because he has looked upon his lowly handmaid.
> Yes, from this day forward all generations will call me blessed,
> for the Almighty has done great things for me.
> Holy is his name, and his mercy reaches from age to age for those who fear him.
> He has shown the power of his arm, he has routed the proud of heart.
> He has pulled down princes from their thrones and exalted the lowly.
> The hungry he has filled with good things, the rich sent empty away.
> He has come to the help of Israel his servant, mindful of his mercy,

according to the promise he made to our ancestors,
of his mercy to Abraham and to his descendants for ever.

Luke 1:46–55

THE LAMB
Love Conquers All

The Lamb that was sacrificed is worthy to be given power, riches, wisdom, strength, honour, glory and blessing.

Apocalypse 5:12

We now come to the heart of the Knock vision, the Lamb, standing on a plain altar, with a large Cross behind it, and angels circling overhead. The witnesses stated that the light shining from the Lamb was greater than that emanating from Mary and the other figures, showing that the Lamb is the focal point of the apparition. What would have gone through the minds of those villagers in 1879 as they gazed upon the Lamb? First of all, for most of these parishioners of a rural farming community, the lamb stood for their livelihood! It is a detail I'm conscious of when preaching on the Good Shepherd, knowing that many in the congregation know a lot more about shepherding sheep than I do. Nevertheless, some of those nineteenth-century witnesses would have also been familiar, at least to some degree, with the theme of the lamb in the Bible, culminating in John the Baptist's exclamation when encountering his cousin Jesus, 'There is the Lamb of God that takes away the sin of the world!' (John 1:39).

We recall Abraham's aforementioned trial of faith, and his prophetic words to his son Isaac, 'God himself will provide the lamb for the burnt offering' (Genesis 22:7–8). We also think of the Passover event of Exodus 12, when the lamb was eaten by the Israelites, and its blood was sprinkled on their doors to protect them from the punishment meted out to the Egyptians. Every Good Friday – the only day of the year when there is no Mass celebrated, anywhere in the world – we hear, during the Celebration of the Lord's Passion, the Fourth Servant Song from Isaiah (52:13–53:12), describing the mysterious servant of the Lord who suffers for his people: 'Harshly dealt with, he bore it humbly, he never opened his mouth, like a lamb that is led to the slaughter-house [...] By his sufferings shall my servant justify many, taking their faults on himself' (53:7, 11). The Church, rereading the First Covenant anew in the light of the Resurrection, understands these passages as all pointing to Jesus, the Messiah (or Anointed One) awaited by his people. Although he was not a great military leader who would deliver his nation by force, as in days of old, he *is* the conquering hero, but in a new, radically different way: by his suffering and death, by being the willing sacrifice to atone for his friends, he delivers and saves, yet in a hidden, mysterious manner that only faith can see.

The Blood of the Covenant

The image of the lamb evokes the gentleness and meekness of Jesus, the Shepherd who becomes the lamb, who 'lays down his life for his sheep' (John 10:11). While he accepts his *passio* – his passive suffering – there is nothing passive in his love for us! Christ makes himself *vulnerable*: his 'power is at its best in weakness'; this must have been a hard lesson to learn for St Paul (as it is for all of us), who goes on to say, 'So I shall be very happy to make my weaknesses my special boast so that the power of Christ may stay over me … for it is when I am weak that I am strong' (2 Corinthians 12:9–10). Here we find an echo of Mary's *Magnificat*, as the poor and lowly are those who have the greatest value in God's eyes. 'For God's foolishness is wiser than human wisdom, and God's weakness is stronger than human strength' (1 Corinthians 1:25). Now if we were looking for an animal which would symbolise a mighty, all-conquering warrior, we probably wouldn't have chosen a lamb; but God's ways are not ours! He wants to reveal his love, understood as a *self-giving love* – he gives himself completely to us, inviting us to give ourselves completely to him: this is the essence of the *covenant*, a family relationship between two partners, not merely a contract or a deal (you give me something, and I'll give you something in return) but an exchange of persons, a sharing of life in mutual love and trust, a sacred bond. This helps us to comprehend something of the greatness of Christian marriage, which St Paul calls a mystery: 'This mystery has many implications, but I am saying that it applies to Christ and the Church' (Ephesians 5:32) – and as every married couple knows, true love means giving of self; true love involves sacrifice! The long biblical account of salvation history that begins with the creation of the man and the woman in the garden (the original meaning of *paradise* in Persian) culminates with a marriage, at the end of the Apocalypse: the wedding feast of the Lamb! So salvation history is a love story, and one with a happy ending. And of course, it's not just those who are married who are called to self-giving love: all of us, whether married or single, can draw inspiration from the burning love of the heavenly Bridegroom, who wants each of us to respond to his beautiful plans for us. Hopefully many contemporary witnesses, who chose to be single lay-persons for the Lord, will be declared saints by the Church, particularly to bring hope and encouragement to those who find themselves single, but not through their own choice.

In the Old Testament, God established various covenants with the human race (successively with Noah, Abraham,

Moses and David) – each of which brought about a new unveiling of his loving plan, his desire to give himself to his children, who would become 'a people set apart to sing the praises of God who called you out of the darkness into his wonderful light' (1 Peter 2:9). Then through the prophets, particularly Jeremiah, he promised a *new covenant*, which would fulfil and surpass all the others, involving a total commitment of himself to his chosen race, in an altogether new way: 'See, the days are coming, when I will make a new covenant with the House of Israel [...] Deep within them I will plant my Law, writing it on their hearts. Then I will be their God and they shall be my people' (Jeremiah 31:31, 33).

So when Jesus, at the Last Supper, says to his disciples, 'This cup is the new covenant in my blood which will be poured out for you' (Luke 22:20), they must have sensed that something special was happening, even if they couldn't grasp or articulate what was going on – a bit like us at Mass sometimes. Jesus, who is about to undergo his supreme sacrifice, 'when he made peace by his death on the cross' (Colossians 1:20), gives them his Body and Blood as their food, something they could never have imagined, bringing the Passover meal – the memorial of how God liberated his people from slavery long ago, when he brought them to the Promised Land – to its fulfilment, yet offering something beyond human comprehension: by this meal, he gives himself completely to them, and shows them the way to the Promised Land of heaven: he himself is the Way!

The Mass

The Knock vision is all about the Mass, and the Cross – we know that the word *Eucharist* means thanksgiving; it is first of all surely a thank you from God, a sign of his gratitude to a nation that had always strived to keep the faith, and to remain faithful to the Mass, despite centuries of persecution and untold suffering. It is a sign of encouragement to us too, as we try to be faithful to his saving gifts in a postmodern, secular age. Many pilgrims find Knock a special place of peace and healing; they often wish they could visit more frequently (and their fervour is a reminder to those of us who live in Knock never to take it for granted) – but every time we go to Mass, wherever we are, we have all we need: we have all the graces of Knock and then some! The liturgy may be celebrated in different fashions – and the Catholic Church has a rich variety of rites and modes of celebration; we can think, for example, of the beautiful Divine Liturgy of St John Chrysostom, of the Greek-Catholics of the Eastern Rite – but however the liturgy is celebrated, every Mass brings heaven to earth in a way that is profound, communitarian and personal.

In the Eucharist, we are brought back to the *past*: to Calvary over two thousand years ago, where we stand, in a way with Mary and John at the foot of the Cross, as the Lamb's loving sacrifice is renewed 'in un-bloody mode', rendering present God's saving actions of long ago. This means that we can not only offer our joys and sorrows, our aches and pains, with his great sacrifice, but also we can seek to console him, to be with him in that dark place as he, the Man of sorrows, is lifted up to draw all to himself.

At the same time, at every Mass we are brought to the *future*: we anticipate the heavenly banquet of the Lamb in glory, where the Lord himself will serve us our supper, and the angels will do the dishes! We are in the presence of the whole Church: united with all our brothers and sisters on earth, as we hear the same Word of God each Sunday (and each weekday) throughout the world, and we receive the one Bread, broken for the life of the world; we glean in faith the presence at Mass of the Holy Souls in purgatory, in some manner, as the Church prays for them, for all who have died, imploring God's mercy for 'those who have died in the peace of your Christ and all the dead, whose faith you alone have known' (Eucharistic Prayer IV). Sometime in the summer of 1879 (probably 13 or 14 May), Archdeacon Bartholomew Kavanagh, parish priest of Knock, decided to offer one hundred consecutive Masses for the Holy Souls; the apparition occurred on the hundredth day – this helps to explain the great devotion to prayer for the deceased in this parish, a tradition which is deeply ingrained in the Irish faithful.

Finally, at every Mass we're in the *present* – or rather, Jesus comes into our present, our now, with all its worries and fears, walking with us on our journey as he walked with the disciples on the road to Emmaus. He often sees us downcast, unable to claim his victory in our situation; he wants our hearts to burn within us on the road, as he explains the Scriptures to us, and he desires us to recognise him in the breaking of Bread (Luke 24:13–35). Christ meets us *on the road* – which means in the midst of our ordinary everyday life, but also with reference to our long journey to the kingdom (he 'comes to hug us on the inside' as a young lad put it to describe his First Holy Communion) to lead us to a different place, to experience something of paradise in our daily lives, with all their brokenness and struggle.

Trinity

The Eucharist is a work of the Holy Trinity. As the Catechism of the Catholic Church explains (1358–81), it can be considered firstly as thanksgiving and praise to the *Father*: through Christ, we can give praise and thanks to God for all that he has done for us, through creation, redemption and sanctification. You know the saying, 'What present can you give to the person who has everything?' There's nothing we can offer to God that he doesn't have already; but like the mum or dad whose child gives them a gift, 'it's the thought that counts', the desire of our hearts to please him which touches him most.

At the same time it is the sacrificial memorial of *Christ* and of his Body, the Church. As we have seen, *memorial* or *remembrance* does not simply mean recalling the past (like retired soccer players reuniting for the anniversary of their cup win, joyful though this may be) but *renders present* what is celebrated: when the Jews celebrate the Passover, the saving events of the Exodus are made real in a certain way; how much more is the one offering of Christ rendered present in the *now*, at every Mass. So whenever the Eucharist is celebrated, the one priestly offering of Christ is continued in time. 'His power to save is utterly certain, since he is living for

ever to intercede for all who come to God through him'
(Hebrews 7:25).

It can also be understood in terms of the presence of
Christ by the power of his Word and the *Holy Spirit*. Jesus
is present to his Church in various ways – in his Word, in
the People of God gathered in prayer, in the poor and the
sick, and in the person of the minister at Mass. But pride
of place is his *real presence* under the eucharistic species,
where *the whole Christ is truly, really and substantially*
contained. Through his Word, spoken through the Church
in the liturgy – during which the Holy Spirit is active in an
eminent way – the bread and wine become Christ's Body
and Blood, given for us and for our salvation.

So the Eucharist is sacrifice, communion and presence –
that's a lot to meditate on! In heaven, we'll have all eternity
to ponder the wonders of the Lord's Eucharistic Love.
In the meantime, however, the Church also offers us the
possibility to pray before the Blessed Sacrament, reserved
in the tabernacle of every church (and often exposed on the
altar in Adoration), which has a strong tradition in various
parts of the world, and which certainly bears fruit in many
ways, visible and invisible. An English bishop, some time
ago, explained how curious he was that a small parish in
his diocese had produced so many priestly vocations, out

of all proportion to its size. He went to check it out, and found that Perpetual Adoration had been practised with great fervour in that parish for many years. As Hercule Poirot might say, this gives one seriously to think!

This recalls the story of a friend of mine – we'll call her Sarah – who had resolved to be baptised, but couldn't decide between the Catholic Church and another Christian community. She found Catholic belief in the Eucharist particularly hard to understand. One night, at a youth festival in a Marian shrine, there was Eucharistic Adoration, so she went along, out of curiosity; it was the middle of the night. When she knelt at the back of the tent and looked at the Host, she saw in it (so she told me) the face of Jesus! So she nudged the young man who was dozing off next to her, with a loud whisper, 'He's there!' The boy woke up, nodded and mumbled, 'Um yeah, he's there' and promptly went back to sleep. So Sarah was baptised into the Catholic Church.

It's good to remember, even when we're dozing off before the Lord, that *he is there*: 'he pours blessings on his beloved while they slumber' (Psalm 126:2). As in the case of another friend of mine – who as a Muslim teenager reading the Gospels under his bedclothes with a torch, had already felt a call to become the Catholic priest he is today – the Holy Spirit is ever at work, and not just in the hearts of those who are already baptised! 'Glory be to him whose power, working in us, can do infinitely more than we can ask or imagine; glory be to him from generation to generation in the Church and in Christ Jesus for ever and ever' (Ephesians 3:20–1).

Resurrection!

The Lamb seen in Knock is *standing* on the altar of sacrifice: this means that he is risen! After the pain and darkness of Good Friday, we have reached the joy of the new dawn of Easter Sunday. By his glorious wounds, we have been healed. Jesus has truly risen from the dead; this is the cornerstone of our faith: 'if our hope in Christ has been for this life only, we are the most unfortunate of all people' (1 Corinthians 15:19). The Lamb has conquered; 'death is swallowed up in victory' (1 Corinthians 15:54). Jesus isn't simply raised from death to go back to his previous life, like those – Jairus' twelve-year-old daughter, the son of the widow of Nain, or Jesus' own friend Lazarus – whom he raised from the dead during his public ministry; they presumably grew old and died in their turn. No, he has been raised by the Father, in the power of the Holy Spirit, to a new kind of life, and he will never die again; as St Paul puts it, he has 'abolished death, and he has proclaimed life and immortality through the Good News' (2 Timothy 1:10). So the Knock apparition contains within it a promise of immortality; death has been vanquished, abolished – this should inspire us to claim the Easter joy and peace given to us as a free gift by the Risen One, for ourselves and all God's children, those living on this earth and all those who have gone before us! However weighed down we might feel sometimes by the troubles of this world, and our own problems, we can give thanks every day for his Resurrection, which is the foretaste and promise of our own resurrection on the last day! Mary can help us experience the joy and peace of this new life; she stood at the foot of the Cross in an abyss of sorrow greater than any of us will ever know, but now she stands – Woman of the Eucharist and Mother of the Resurrection – rejoicing with the Lamb, for he has won the victory and every tear will be wiped away. When we go into the Apparition Chapel in Knock, or any other church, when we are at home or on the road, wherever we are, we can participate in this joy of the Resurrection, in company with the radiant exultation of the saints in heaven, our brothers and sisters who await us with so much love and anticipation.

Funerals involve the whole community in rural Ireland; work stops, just about everyone attends the removal or the funeral Mass, and often both. We priests try to find words appropriate for the solemn occasion, seeking to balance the need to pray for the dead with God's promise of heaven. I was somewhat disconcerted by Fr Paddy's way of preaching at a funeral Mass I was concelebrating: already in his mid-eighties, he was almost dancing with delight at the lectern; 'I *know* I'm going to heaven, I can't wait!' was the essence of his homily. From anyone else, it might have bordered on presumption, but seeing this elderly priest glowing with living faith and expectant hope, you sensed that God wouldn't dare to disappoint him. He died not long afterwards; one can trust there was a lively celebration when he reached the goal of his hope!

The Gardener

'Woman, why are you weeping?' (John 20:13, 15) Mary of Magdala was there at the Cross; her beloved Lord, the one who had delivered her from seven demons, had been put to death, and all hope had ended. She came to the garden to anoint his body, but they had apparently taken him away. So she stays near the tomb, weeping (modern French still has the phrase *pleurer comme une madeleine*, 'to cry like a Magdalene') – and Jesus comes to meet her. Yet something prevents her from recognising him: she supposes him to be the gardener! In a way, she's right: he is the divine Gardener who established our first parents in the garden of Eden, where they enjoyed bodily immortality and freedom from suffering – until they chose to disobey God. Happily, through the obedience of the New Man, 'even to accepting death, death on a cross' (Philippians 2:8), even greater gifts than those enjoyed by Adam and Eve before the Fall are offered to the whole human race: eternal life in the vision of God, face to face; bliss beyond all human experience or imagination; an ever-increasing joy and love shared and magnified among all the redeemed. And now, in a garden, Jesus meets this woman who will be heralded by the whole Church as *Apostle to the Apostles* (and whose memorial day was upgraded by Pope Francis to the status of Feast during the Year of Mercy, highlighting the work of the Lord's mercy in her). He calls her by name – 'Mary' – and then she recognises him. But he does not want her to cling to him, he immediately gives her a mission: 'Go and find the brothers, and tell them: I am ascending to my Father and your Father, to my God and your God' (John 20:17). Jesus knows each of us by our name, he comes to encounter us in our sadness, inviting us to look at him, to meet his gaze and therein to find hope and joy. He gives each of us a mission, which might be something quite humble and apparently insignificant, simply to perform our daily tasks, but with a new vigour and desire to share the Good News with those he places on our path. Through his Passover, his 'passing over' through the veil which separates us from the kingdom, his Father is now ours, his God is our God. And because the Temple veil was torn from top to bottom (Mark 15:38), we gain access to the Holy of Holies, the new garden, yet already we can live as sons and daughters of the Father, children of the kingdom.

A good way to banish the blues is to read the last chapter (or last two chapters in John) of each of the four Gospels, the Resurrection accounts; it won't take long, and will help us to meet the Risen One in our need, and serve to remind us of his plans for our lives and his beautiful dreams for our eternity. An event cited above, on the road to Emmaus (Luke 24:13–35), is a particularly helpful aid to meeting the Lord: those two rather depressed disciples were walking away from Jerusalem (the holy city, a key theme in Luke); they had seen their aspirations completely shattered by the Cross, and found themselves bereft of all hope. All of us may experience this kind of feeling at some point in our lives; disappointment and failure are inevitable aspects of the human condition, but what may seem even worse for the believer is when we trusted that God was guiding us in a certain direction, and it only led to a dead end! As the psalmist sighed long ago, 'I said, "This is what causes my grief; that the way of the Most High has changed"' (Psalm 76:11). So what does Jesus do? He walks alongside them, as a friend on the journey; again, they don't recognise him, but 'he explained to them the passages throughout the scriptures that were about himself' (24:27) and their hearts are burning within them. Then, having been gradually uplifted in spirit by this mysterious stranger, they do something crucial: they invite him to stay with them. Then he takes bread, which will be *blessed*, *broken* and *given* – as the Lamb was, to save us, and as we shall be, to share in his work of redemption. Now they recognise him 'but he had vanished from their sight' (24:31). Just when we think we've taken possession of the Lord, he vanishes! Because now we, like the disciples on the way to Emmaus, have to live in faith. They at once set out toward Jerusalem – it must be dark by now, but they are filled with light and joy – to share their story with the Eleven: 'what had happened on the road and how they had recognised him at the breaking of bread' (24:35).

The Emmaus encounter is the Mass in a nutshell: we begin by acknowledging our helpless state when left to our own devices; we then hear the Word of God, allowing Jesus to explain it to us through the priest or deacon (we preachers do our best, but we can't guarantee our listeners' hearts will burn as we share the word! All of us should call on the Holy Spirit to inspire those who preach and those who listen) – and finally, we recognise him at the breaking of bread, as we receive the Word made flesh in Holy Communion. It's important to affirm that we receive, at every Eucharist, the *risen, glorified* Body of the Lord, his pure risen Heart of love! So part of us is already raised, this is why St Paul can exclaim, 'now the life you have is hidden with Christ in God' (Colossians 3:1). *My life is hidden with Christ in God* – isn't that a blessed thought we can whisper to ourselves now and then? Even if we don't grasp its full meaning, we understand that something in us is already in heaven with Jesus; our room has been prepared, it's got our name on the door, and no one can take it from us, if we keep trusting and hoping.

Revelation

'The throne of God and of the Lamb will be in its place in the city; his servants will worship him, they will see him face to face and his name will be written on their foreheads. It will never be night again and they will not need lamplight or sunlight, because the Lord God will be shining on them. They will reign for ever and ever' (Apocalypse 22:3–5).

It would be fitting to make a thorough analysis of the Apocalypse (the Book of Revelation) in the light of the Knock apparition, but that would require a book in itself. We note that the *Lamb who was slain* is at the centre of John's visions at Patmos – the word 'lamb' (singular or plural) appears some 38 times in the New Testament, of which 29 occur in the Apocalypse. The challenging last book of the Bible is hard to interpret, but can be summed up as follows: the Lamb has won the victory, and it is the victory of his self-giving Love. The Lamb is *worthy*: worthy to open the scroll (which would appear to symbolise the fulfilling of God's plans), worthy to receive glory and kingship and every honour, *because* he was sacrificed (Apocalypse 4–5) – in other words, because of his passionate love for each one of us which led him to give his life for us, he conquers sin and death. All those who followed him on the painful way of the Cross are invited to share his glory with him.

'If you believe, you will see the glory of God' (John 11:40); in a way, the marble vision representing the event of 1879 makes it easier for us to believe. We draw from the faith experience of so many who have prayed before us in this blessed spot, and we live in hope that we will see his glory, the glory of the Lamb, the one who is faithful, far more faithful than we can ever be.

A Praise Litany

We can conclude with my favourite Praise Litany, which can be recited before the Blessed Sacrament, to help us when we don't have adequate words to give the Lamb of God the praise he deserves:

> My Jesus, I believe in you – Praise you, Jesus!
> My Jesus, I hope in you – Praise you, Jesus!
> My Jesus, I trust in you – Praise you, Jesus!
> My Jesus, I thank you – Praise you, Jesus!
> My Jesus, I bless you – Praise you, Jesus!
> My Jesus, I love you – Praise you, Jesus!
> My Jesus, I adore you – Praise you, Jesus!

CONCLUSION

A New Creation

Then I saw a new heaven and a new earth; the first heaven and the first earth had disappeared now, and there was no longer any sea. I saw the holy city, the new Jerusalem, coming down from God out of heaven, as beautiful as a bride all dressed for her husband. Then I heard a loud voice call from the throne, 'You see this city? Here God lives among men. He will make his home among them; they shall be his people, and he will be their God; his name is God-with-them. He will wipe away all tears from their eyes; there will be no more death, and no more mourning or sadness. The world of the past has gone.' Then the One sitting on the throne spoke: 'Now I am making the whole of creation new,' he said.

Apocalypse 21:1–5

Home is where the heart is

It's good to come back home after a trip, especially when you've been away a long time. For some, it might be the family home, that contains many happy memories; for others instead, it would be a place they felt an affinity with, even if far from their origins – for some of us, a place such as Knock becomes a home, because that's where we've found something that seems to correspond to the deepest yearnings of our hearts.

Many people, especially those who've lived outside of their own country for some length of time, don't really have a place they can call home – to say nothing of refugees, victims of war and famine, all those who are forced to leave for a strange land, obliged to find a 'somewhere', anywhere to live. I knew a man from Poland, who was forced to flee his land after World War II; he settled in Paris, where he lived for nearly sixty years, yet never really felt settled. As an old man, he was able to return to his native Warsaw (which he'd not even been able to visit all those years): upon arrival, he said, 'I feel at home for the first time in sixty years!' He died some time later, finally at home.

What do we need to feel at home? What do we need to be happy? This query is actually in Scripture: '"What can bring us happiness?" many say' (Psalm 4:7). Once a little boy was sad, because his pet dog had died. He asked a wise old priest, 'Will my dog be in heaven?' The priest smiled. He replied, 'If you need your dog for you to be happy in heaven, he'll be there with you.' That little boy was my own late father, so this conversation must have happened around 1930 – I never heard a better response to this perennial question. Now we could make a wish list of our dream cottage, the perfect spot to live (if only we won the lottery), our ideal pet and nice neighbours, and yet … it might not be enough to make us happy. Home is where the heart is, that's so true – yet there is good news for the many who don't feel an affinity with any particular place in our world: in heaven, we will feel more at home than anywhere we could call home on this earth! Everything will be just right; the Father's house has many rooms. The holy city will be filled with light and joy – and there'll be beautiful gardens, countryside, lakes and rivers, all we could wish for, all we ever longed to enjoy – and there'll be no need for cell phones or car insurance, burglar alarms or stain remover. 'You are no longer aliens or foreign visitors; you are citizens like all the saints, and part of God's household' (Ephesians 2:19).

So heaven will surpass our deepest yearnings for 'home', a zillion times (I'm not sure how much a zillion is, but it's a big number). Even if we imagined the greatest wish list possible, heaven would be infinitely more wonderful. St Paul puts it like this: 'the things that no eye has seen and no ear has heard, things beyond the mind of man, all that God has prepared for those who love him: these are the very things that God has revealed to us through the Spirit' (1 Corinthians 2:9–10).

God has revealed these things through the Spirit, to those who love him: through his Word and Church teaching, he reveals – but as he knows we need 'extras', he is free to reveal something more of the glory of heaven whenever he wishes, to those who seek him in love. This brings us to the Knock apparition: a revelation of heaven, made to humble people in a neglected region of a small country on the edge of Europe, *but a people who loved him*. We can feel at home in the Shrine chapel before the beautiful statues of the vision by Lorenzo Ferri – or in the renovated Basilica, contemplating the spectacular mosaic produced from a design by P.J. Lynch, unveiled in 2016 – because heaven has come close to us, to speak to us about God's sacrificial love.

We seem to find a common theme running through Scripture, very much in harmony with the message of Knock: the paradox of how God wins through defeat, brings life from death, makes the poor and lowly into kings, and shows his power in and through our weakness. The meek, defenceless Lamb, led to the slaughterhouse, triumphs over the powers of evil; so, in their turn, will his disciples, lowly and insignificant though they may be in the eyes of the world, which is drawn insatiably to all that glitters, be victorious over all the dark forces that threaten society today. The Lamb's invitation to be 'givers' of love in return for his total self-giving for us goes against the grain of much of modern culture, which urges us frenetically to be 'takers', consumers: look out for number one, take it easy, 'spend, spend, spend'. God's call to authentic love does impel us to 'spend', but rather to spend ourselves in the service of others! John Paul II liked to quote a key phrase from Vatican II: the human person 'cannot fully find himself except through a sincere gift of himself' (*Gaudium et Spes*, 24). And Mother Teresa suggested the path to true joy, as an acronym: Jesus, Others, Yourself – if we live with our priorities in that order, we'll be truly blessed. Of course, it's easier said than done, that's why we need God's grace and the constant reminder of Jesus, 'Cut off from me, you can do nothing' (John 15:5), but which is completed by St Paul: 'There is nothing I cannot master with the help of the One who gives me strength' (Philippians 4:13). So Knock is very much for our times; it is at once a call to prayer, to Mass and Marian devotion, but above all an affirmation that self-giving love conquers all.

A friend of mine once gave me a present, saying, 'It's what you preach about in your homilies, Padre.' I could see it was something to eat. This friend is a bit of a joker, so I was expecting fudge, or maybe waffle – but it was a box of chocolates called 'Heaven'! A reminder that we can and must 'preach heaven', or even better, witness by our lives to the fact that there *is* a heaven – not 'pie in the sky when you die' as a comforting thought to evade our current painful state – but a wonderful reality, where, after our final purification from all that is not true love, we will be face to face with the One who chose us before the world was made, in perfect communion with many new friends, with no more tears or mourning. Every charitable action and selfless deed will be uncovered and celebrated; every effort for the good and the true will be rewarded. Above all, the joy of being loved, infinitely beyond any earthly imaginings, and being able to return love for love, will be multiplied among the saints ever more throughout the kingdom. As Fr Paddy would say, 'I can't wait!'

What you have come to is Mount Zion and the city of the living God, the heavenly Jerusalem where the millions of angels have gathered for the festival, with the whole Church in which everyone is a first-born son and a citizen of heaven. You have come to God himself, the supreme Judge, and been placed with the spirits of the saints who have been made perfect; and to Jesus, the mediator who brings a new covenant and a blood for purification which pleads more insistently than Abel's.

Hebrews 12:22–4

The Secret

To sum up, the secret of the Knock Apparition is manifold. It affirms our redemption by the Cross and Resurrection of Christ, the Lamb of God, who is in his own flesh our gateway to heaven. It presents his closest friends, who seem each in their turn to reflect in a particular way one of the Persons of the Holy Trinity. St Joseph shows us how we can become merciful like the Father, while St John encourages us to live as a beloved son or daughter, as a true child of God. And Mary, Bride of the Spirit and Woman of the Eucharist, shines out for us as she stands beside our crosses, imparting to us the faith and the hope she lived to the utmost on this earth, so that we can experience the joy of the resurrection and a new Pentecost of love, in the Holy Spirit.

Knock opens up the Mass for us, inviting us to live the Eucharist as our *viaticum*, the food we need on our way to the kingdom: 'Get up and eat, or the journey will be too long for you,' as the angel said to Elijah (1 Kings 19:7). There were angels in Knock too, to remind us of their gentle presence and powerful protection in our lives; they were adoring the Lamb and inviting us to do the same. Speaking of angels … when I first came to work part-time in Knock, I took the bus each week from Galway. One particular day, I realised I'd forgotten to bring enough money for the bus back. We'll see what Providence brings, I muttered. It happened that the next morning, I was on early Mass at the Carmelite convent. I 'trudged doggedly' (to use Tolkien's wonderful phrase) through the freezing fog – it was late September. I quickly overtook a little lady (whom I'd never seen in my life) hobbling with a stick, heading for the convent. As I passed her, she handed me an envelope with my name on it, saying, 'There's a Mass offering for you, Father, and a little extra.' I had my bus fare. I asked her for her name – it was Angela. It was the Feast of the Archangels.

As well as the Eucharist, Bread of angels, all the *sacraments* – saving actions which are signs and instruments of communion between God and his beloved children, between heaven and earth – are at least implied in the Knock event, since they all come from Christ and bring us to him. *Baptism* is indicated by St John the Baptist being the patron saint of Knock parish church. *Confirmation* is implicit in the presence of St John the Evangelist since he was one of the apostles on whom Christ breathed after his Resurrection, saying 'Receive the Holy Spirit' (John 20:20); John the Apostle also witnesses to the ministerial *priesthood*, instituted by Christ the Lord himself. St Joseph and Mary stand there together to help and inspire man and woman united in holy *marriage* – which is itself a sign of God's betrothing all of us to himself at the wedding-feast of the Lamb in heaven. Finally, Jesus is the Lamb who takes away our sins, and mandates his priests to do this for each of us personally through the sacrament of *reconciliation*: 'those whose sins you forgive, they are forgiven' (John 20:21); he also sends out his priests to impart *anointing* to the sick and the dying, for 'he took our sicknesses away and carried our diseases for us' (Matthew 8:16; see also James 5:14).

The last two sacraments mentioned – reconciliation and anointing – are key elements of a pilgrimage to Knock; there we can be sure that miracles of grace at work, mostly known to God alone; the Father's mercy comes to meet us in our struggle with sin and sickness. The Chapel of Reconciliation in Knock has been open for over a quarter of a century: if its walls could talk, they would surely praise God's compassion and healing! When we pluck up the courage go to confession, we're like the prodigal son coming home, bruised and battered by our mistakes and wrong turns, yet the Father waits longingly for us, moved with pity, and prepares a celebration, since his beloved child 'was dead and has come back to life, was lost and is found' (Luke 15:24).

We've still only begun to unpack the full meaning of God's message to us through Knock; to use an image borrowed from St Augustine, it's like a well from which we can drink abundantly without it ever running dry. What those witnesses saw long ago as a great light on a wet Thursday night is still a light for us today; 'a light that shines in the dark' (John 1:5). And wherever the darkness appears to gain the upper hand, the more the light will shine out.'What we are waiting for is what he promised: the new heavens and new earth, the place where righteousness will be at home' (2 Peter 3:13).

This love revealed

Like the Eucharist itself, the apparition is all about sacrifice, communion and presence. The One who loved us offered himself in *sacrifice* for us, yearning for us to give him ourselves in return. He is the bridge between heaven and earth, enabling us to live in *communion* with him and with our brothers and sisters, on earth as in heaven. And he reveals his *presence* among his people, for he is God-with-us! He will never leave us, for he has promised, 'I am with you always, yes, to the end of time' (Matthew 28:20). May all those who visit Knock experience his love for them, a love which is always new, a love which transforms us into a new creation. May all pilgrims be renewed in hope, carrying back home with them this love revealed, so that the love which conquers might spread through the whole world.

'How rich are the depths of God – how deep his wisdom and knowledge – and how impossible to penetrate his motives or understand his methods! Who could ever know the mind of the Lord? Who could ever be his counsellor? Who could ever give him anything or lend him anything? All that exists comes from him; all is by him and for him. To him be glory for ever!' (Romans 11:33–6)

Appendix

Novena Prayer to Our Lady of Knock

In the name of the Father, and of the Son, and of the Holy Spirit. Amen.

Give praise to the Father almighty,
to his Son, Jesus Christ the Lord,
to the Spirit who lives in our hearts,
both now and forever. Amen.

Our Lady of Knock, Queen of Ireland,
you gave hope to your people in a time of distress, and comforted them in sorrow.
You have inspired countless pilgrims to pray with confidence to your divine Son,
remembering His promise,
'Ask and you shall receive, seek and you shall find.'

Help me to remember that we are all pilgrims on the road to heaven.

Fill me with love and concern for my brothers and sisters in Christ,

especially those who live with me.

Comfort me when I am sick, lonely or depressed.

Teach me how to take part ever more reverently in the Holy Mass.

Give me a greater love of Jesus in the Blessed Sacrament.

Pray for me now, and at the hour of my death. Amen.

Lamb of God, you take away the sins of the world; have mercy on us.

Lamb of God, you take away the sins of the world; have mercy on us.

Lamb of God, you take away the sins of the world; grant us peace.

St Joseph, chosen by God to be the husband of Mary,

the protector of the Holy Family,

the guardian of the Church,

protect all families in their work and recreation

And guard us on our journey through life.

Lamb of God, you take away the sins of the world; have mercy on us.

Lamb of God, you take away the sins of the world; have mercy on us.

Lamb of God, you take away the sins of the world; grant us peace.

St John, beloved disciple of the Lord,
faithful priest,
teacher of the Word of God,
help us to hunger for the Word,
to be loyal to the Mass,
and to love one another.

Lamb of God, you take away the sins of the world; have mercy on us.

Lamb of God, you take away the sins of the world; have mercy on us.

Lamb of God, you take away the sins of the world; grant us peace.

Our Lady of Knock, pray for us
Refuge of Sinners, pray for us
Queen Assumed into Heaven, pray for us

Queen of the Rosary, pray for us
Mother of Nazareth, pray for us
Queen of Virgins, pray for us
Help of Christians, pray for us
Health of the Sick, pray for us
Queen of Peace, pray for us
Our Lady, Queen and Mother, pray for us
Our Lady, Mother of the Church, pray for us

(*Here mention your own special intentions*)

With the Angels and Saints let us pray:

Give praise to the Father almighty,
to his Son, Jesus Christ the Lord,
to the Spirit who lives in our hearts,
both now and forever.
Amen.

Knock Shrine official website: www.knock-shrine.ie
To contact the author, email: nigel.woollen@gmail.com